EARN IT, OWN IT

EARN IT, OWN IT

The Disruptive Agency Model Where Top
Insurance Producers Are Finding Freedom,
Wealth, and Their Dream Life

———

BRUCE JOHNSON

LIONCREST
PUBLISHING

This book was prepared and authored by Bruce Johnson in his personal capacity. The opinions expressed are the author's own and do not necessarily reflect the views of the Insurance Office of America or its Board of Directors.

EARN IT, OWN IT
The Disruptive Agency Model Where Top Insurance Producers
Are Finding Freedom, Wealth, and Their Dream Life

ISBN   978-1-5445-1091-0 *Paperback*
        978-1-5445-1092-7 *Ebook*
        978-1-5445-1093-4 *Audiobook*

This book is dedicated to all the amazing people in the IOA family. To my brothers and sisters across the globe who show up and step up every day and selflessly serve our producers, clients, and carrier partners. You all make IOA an extremely special place. Without you, none of this works. And because of you, we have been not only recognized as the best company to partner with in the insurance industry, but also as the absolute best company to work for.

CONTENTS

PREFACE

Someone said a long time ago that everyone has at least one book in them. In other words, we all have a story to tell. In my case, I've chosen to share with you one of the best decisions I've ever made in my life. My name is Bruce Johnson, and eighteen years ago, I decided to pursue an opportunity that's enabled me to succeed in business at a level far beyond what I had thought possible. It's also enabled me to provide for my family, to help others, and to live an unscripted life of freedom and abundance.

Whether you're a commercial insurance producer, an agency owner, or someone considering a career in insurance sales, this book is for you. Even if this specific opportunity doesn't turn out to be a good fit, I hope you can take something away that will improve your business or help in your life.

You won't hear about this opportunity from any agency

owner, public agency executive, or job recruiter. It's simply not in their best interest for this information to get out. If pressed directly, they will usually tell you, "It sounds too good to be true," or "It will never last." Well, that's what I thought at first too.

You see, the typical corporate insurance agency (or corporate model) is set up with an owner or a few owners at the top who own everything and make most of the money. In public agencies, the stockholders demand annual profits and continuous growth in share value. It's in their best interest to keep this gravy train rolling without disruption.

In this book, I will introduce you to a revolutionary agency model that was designed to take the greed out of the insurance business and to share the wealth. It's called the Entrepreneurial Model and was created by visionary entrepreneur and super producer, John Ritenour, after his boss thought it would be a good idea to reduce his commissions three times within a nine-month period.

John, along with his wife, Valli, started Insurance Office of America (IOA) with three employees and a vision that every producer would become an owner and partner in the company. Instead of middle management, the producers would each contribute to running the company. In exchange, they would receive the highest commissions in the industry (up to 57 percent) for both new *and* renewal business. And, they would have ownership in their book of business—creating freedom and financial prosperity that was pretty much unheard of for most producers.

The staff employees would also have the opportunity to become owners in the company through a generous employee stock ownership (ESOP) program. And most importantly, the cornerstone or foundation of this new agency would be faith, family, and the fun of living their lifework.

Insurance Office of America was created in response and as an alternative to the corporate insurance agency model. In the words of founder and chairman, John Ritenour, spoken at IOA's 2017 national sales meeting:

> "I knew what I wasn't getting at that other agency, and I knew what I wanted. I felt like I needed to do something different, so I cast a vision of five values:
>
> 1. I wanted to take the greed out of the insurance agency business.
> 2. I wanted to share the wealth with all the producers and employees.
> 3. I wanted book equity.
> 4. I wanted new and renewal commissions to be the same.
> 5. And, I wanted the producers and employees to have stock ownership.

"The last goal I came up with, and this wasn't until a little later—after I set the first five goals, I wanted to make this company generational. When I moved from Pittsburgh to Florida, I sold my agency to a guy who worked for me for quite a while, somebody I trusted dearly, and he was going to pay me out over six years. Six months later, he quit paying me. I had to make a choice: do I go back to Pittsburgh, or do I stay here and build this? Well, I stayed. Thank God.

"I could have gone back and probably made a good living, but thank God, I'm in Florida and thank God, we built this company.

"When we first started, I was thinking we would be a local success. But God had a better plan than I did, because now we're much more than a local success, thanks to everyone in the organization.

"All of this happened because two kids from Pittsburgh took a shot. It wasn't easy. It took a lot of faith, hard work, and sacrifices. I worked day and night, and so did [my wife] Valli. We'd go coach in the afternoon and then go clean office buildings at night. We sacrificed to make sure this thing was going to work.

"When I started IOA—Insurance Office of Florida at the time—I borrowed $10,000 to start the company.

Thank God the bank was so stupid, and they gave me a loan.

"Those initial values I came up with set the tone to do something way more than I ever dreamed of because it started to build a culture. A culture of all those values rolled into one, in a place where people wanted to be—not handcuffed. If you want to leave, go out and take your shot. I did. So, when you're building a company like this, you have to give people the freedom to do what Valli and I did.

"We're still early in this, and the second generation of leadership has taken over (with Heath Ritenour as CEO and Jeff Lagos as president), and it's going to bless people much greater than I ever did. There's going to be a lot of millionaires built out of IOA, including the staff who support our customers and take care of us (not just the producers).

The thing I'm most proud of is my son, Heath, who has stepped into my shoes and has done an unbelievable job of taking over IOA, making it way better than I ever could. The future of IOA is in great hands."

One of the things everyone is most proud of at IOA is that we look nothing like a traditional insurance agency, or any other agency for that matter.

We have a CEO, a president, and a board of directors like other agencies. But here, all but a few of the board members are successful producers in the trenches just like us. They give a tremendous amount of their time to make IOA a better place.

We lead by serving and putting the needs of others first. Whether to our customers, our staff, or our carrier partners, we believe the more we give, the more others will become empowered and engaged in our common mission of serving the greater good. We're not policy peddlers. We advocate for our clients and view ourselves as sharing a seat at the table with their other trusted advisors, like their attorney or CPA, for example.

It's also the only agency I know of where every producer has the opportunity to out-earn the CEO!

IOA is a global company with a small company feel. Our culture is supportive of our obligations to our families, which includes taking time off work to spend with our children, attend important events, be with loved ones if they're sick, or do whatever we need to do in order to be there for them.

We believe in God first, family second, and work third.

For those of you who may be thinking like I initially did,

that, "This model sounds too good to be true; it will never last," consider this: today, IOA has more than 1,000 associates in more than fifty branch offices in the US and London. As one of the nation's fastest-growing insurance agencies, it was recently ranked twenty-fourth in *Business Insurance's* list of largest brokers and ranked twelfth on *Insurance Journal's* Top 100 Independent Property/Casualty agencies report.

The more one digs in and does their research, it becomes apparent that this disruptive company is here to stay and has only begun to scratch the surface of its true potential. This producer and employee-owned company is poised to more than double in size over the next five years. Unlike most national and regional brokers who rely on acquisitions to sustain their growth, most of IOA's unprecedented growth has been organic, generated internally by their producer/owners growing their books, and by adding quality, like-minded producers who grew tired of corporate greed and wanted to build something they could own and be proud of. IOA's organic growth is more than two times the industry average of public and private equity-owned firms. Their producer retention is 94 percent and their client retention is 96 percent.

As CEO, Heath Ritenour frequently says, "Today is the smallest that IOA will ever be."

Heath continues, "I know I've said it before, but I've never felt so strongly about what I'm about to say. We're only at the tip of the iceberg of where we're going. The caliber of quality partners joining IOA gets better every year. And as this message gets out about how truly different we are, the floodgates are just going to bust open. But, we're going to do it the right way. We're going to be picky, and we're going to bring in partners who fit, and people we can all be proud to call our partners. People who just make us better."

For any producer who may be kicking the tires or considering their options, IOA is just getting started, and there is still time to get in on the ground floor of this life-changing opportunity.

Best of all, IOA will *never* be up for sale. Heath gets calls almost every week from large brokers, private equity firms, and other people who want to buy IOA. His answer is always the same, "IOA is not and will never be for sale. The answer is not only no, but hell no!"

If you would like to learn more, I invite you to continue reading about this real-life American success story that has been a difference-maker in the lives of so many, including the lives of IOA producers, their families, their staff, and their insurance carrier partners.

MY BACKGROUND AND WHY I JOINED IOA

Eighteen years ago, I was doing fairly well as a commercial producer with a large corporate insurance agency in Tampa, Florida. It was a quality agency with a good reputation and a great group of people. While I was comfortable, it seemed like something was missing. I wasn't excited about going to work every day and was even less excited about the mandatory weekly sales meeting. I was also playing it safe. While I probably could have sustained an average or above average career there, it wouldn't have been the robust life I really wanted.

I'd been there about four years, hitting my meager sales goal each year, which was only about $50,000 in new revenue (not very demanding). One day my boss called me into his office—a large corner office in a downtown high-rise overlooking the Tampa skyline. While he'd always treated me fairly, the situation was still a little intimidating. You see, my boss was a super sharp and successful corporate CEO. He stood six-feet-seven, had silver hair, and wore a perfectly tailored suit every day. I couldn't help but feel a little nervous.

We sat down at a corner table and reviewed my latest numbers. Then, we mutually agreed there was no reason my new goal shouldn't be $100,000 in new revenue. It really wasn't a topic for debate. We both knew I had some potential, and I definitely received the message loud and clear that my new business production would need to be $100,000 in new revenue every year going forward.

I'd heard about IOA and had been pondering it in the back of my mind for some time prior to that meeting. So, when I realized I was going to have to ramp up to hit this new goal anyway, I thought, "Why not do it at IOA? I could be making more than what I'm making now within about two years, I'd have equity in my book, and I'd have complete control over my time and my future." I was tired of making money for others while I was simply making ends meet.

One reason I'd been reluctant to join when I first heard about IOA was that it sounded too good to be true. I wasn't sure the promises would stand the test of time. But they were opening new offices, and when they opened one in my home city of Tampa, it began to seem like a viable option. Bill Massaro, a local producer I had known and respected for many years, had recently joined IOA and was put in charge of growing the Tampa office, so I contacted him and arranged a meeting.

Over lunch, he asked me a lot of questions and told me about his story and why he had joined IOA. He also explained how everything worked and answered all of my questions. By the end of that lunch, I had made my decision and was beyond fired up to make the move. All that was left was to get the blessing of the founder, John

Ritenour, who approved everyone who came on board in those earlier days.

I nervously made the two-hour drive to Altamonte Springs to meet with John. You see, I'd already decided to burn my bridges and join IOA no matter what it took. I was all in and 100 percent committed to doing this. But, I didn't know John. What if he rejected me? It would suck, and I'd have to come up with another plan.

For whatever reason, John decided to give me a shot. I'm not sure if he actually saw some potential or took pity on me. Either way, I didn't care. I was officially in, and it was the best feeling in the world!

Starting over at IOA meant starting completely from scratch; I would have to start building my book one account at a time. This didn't bother me too much because I wasn't crushing it financially anyway. I had also recently divorced for the second time and was starting my personal life over again, so in a sense, it was pretty good timing. I looked at the entire transition as sort of a clean slate and wondered how I was going to script my life going forward. I wondered about the kind of life I really wanted to have.

One thing was clear: it was up to me.

So, rather than overthink it, I just put my head down and

started grinding away, hardly ever looking up. I made a little more progress every day. I focused on hitting singles and doubles, simply trying to survive and build a solid base. After three short years, I was making more than my former income and enjoying my newly earned freedom.

It was eighteen years ago when I made that fateful decision to bet on myself and join IOA, and I've never looked back. Today, I'm making more than seven times what I was making in that prior job. In addition, I have equity in my book of business, which just surpassed my long-term goal of $1 million in revenue. No doubt, my finances are looking pretty good, and I don't mean to brag or anything. Lord knows, there are many people much smarter and way more successful than I will ever be. I'm just trying to illustrate what's possible for a regular person who's willing to put in some relentless hard work and take a shot.

I now have complete control of my time and money. I wake up every morning and pinch myself—feeling truly blessed that this is my life. I have no boss waiting for me at the office. I can play hooky or hit the beach if I want. Instead, I usually wake around 5:00 a.m., eat a clean breakfast, and then enjoy some coffee while taking in the amazing water view from our balcony. Then I'll organize my plan for the day, make calls, or send emails from my remote home office, check in with my awesome team at IOA to see if they need anything, and then I head out to work on my business. I also hit the gym most days; sometimes it's during lunch and other times, it's in the afternoon. It doesn't really matter because I don't need anyone's permission. I just go whenever it fits into my schedule for that day. In addition to my faith, exercise is an awesome stress reliever. It's one of the things that helps keep me balanced and focused on what's really important.

To me, what's most important is family. Well, that and also the practice of giving back and helping others. The Bible says in Luke 12:48, "To unto whomsoever much is given, of him shall much be required."

In the past, I was never in this position nor had this opportunity. It's an amazing feeling to help others and make a difference in someone's life. When we take the focus off "me" and place it on others, it's truly incredible the doors that God will open up.

You see, the motivation for me is different now. I hustle because I want to, because I choose to, and because I've been blessed to be part of this amazing company that allows me to.

PLAN FOR THE UNEXPECTED

While none of us can predict what will happen in the future, there are three things we can reliably count on and should definitely plan for. Those are death, taxes, and corporations acting in the best interest of their owners or shareholders. Here are a few stories that hit close to home for me.

BRUCE'S STORY

This story is about another Bruce. Before becoming a multimillion-dollar revenue producer and a regional president of IOA, Bruce Eades worked in Gainesville, Georgia, as a vice president and producer for a large national brokerage that was eventually sold to Willis. He had been doing well with the company for about eight years and had built a solid book of business along with great client relationships.

Then, one day, all of that changed.

As corporations will do from time to time, some "genius" in the ivory tower made the brilliant decision to hire a new manager to shake things up and crack the whip on the sales team. He reasoned that a new sheriff would bring a no-nonsense attitude to the operation, and sales would increase.

Well, he did shake things up in a sense, but not in a good way. By clamping down and taking away their freedom and flexibility, the staff felt like they were working for a tyrant. In fact, the team gave him an affectionate and fitting nickname that won't be repeated here, but Bruce might share it if you ask.

This new manager ended up having the opposite effect leadership had intended. Morale in the office was so bad that producers started polishing their resumes instead of focusing on their sales goals. As Bruce explains, "This guy came in and stole the team's freedom." He sucked the soul right out of the place they all loved and had dedicatedly worked for so many years.

Shortly thereafter, management announced a commission cut and declared they would be taking away smaller accounts. At the time, there weren't many accounts in Bruce's territory generating over $10,000 in revenue. In one fell swoop, the company unilaterally was changing the rules of the game without offering any discussion on the matter.

Bruce was looking at a significant cut to his pay, his security, and his lifestyle. It happened overnight, and was completely out of his control.

SANDY'S STORY

A few years ago, one of the nation's largest insurance brokers made an announcement that shocked the industry.

OK, maybe shocked is an exaggeration, but it sure dealt a devastating blow to the company's producer sales force. It changed their lives as they had known them up to that point. The company declared that, going forward, the agency would no longer be paying commissions on any account generating less than $10,000 in revenue. That's right, any account generating less than $10,000 in revenue from that point forward would be serviced by a dedicated small business unit with no producer involvement.

When the news hit the street, one of my partners and I wasted no time inviting one of their local producers, Sandy, out for lunch (not her real name). We were eager to find out what was happening over there and get her take on how she and the other producers were handling the new deal. We also thought this might present an opportunity to pick up a great producer or two amid the chaos.

Sandy did some quick math and realized that with one stroke of the greedy corporate pen, her annual income would fall from about $150,000 to less than $50,000 overnight. This was mainly because a large portion of her accounts fell into the "under $10,000" range. Most of the relationships she'd spent time building and cultivating over the last twenty-four years were being wiped out. They were being reduced to just numbers on a commission statement. If the number was below $10,000, the account would go to the service center. How would she explain to her clients that they could no longer work with her? After all, these were people who relied on Sandy. She was not only their trusted advisor, but many also considered her a friend. For Sandy, it felt like she was being punched in the gut, and there wasn't anything she could do about it. Like Bruce, her income, her security, and her lifestyle were about to radically change due to something out of her control. The rules of the game had changed with little advance notice and entirely without her input.

Unfortunately, blind directives like this are not unusual in the corporate model. Because corporate agencies answer to owners or shareholders and not to the agency's employees or producers, they can change the rules of the game whenever they deem it to be in their best interest.

In the case of Sandy's employer, one could speculate that they were just sprucing up the financials in preparation for their recently announced sale. In other cases, management would make cuts prior to year-end in order to hit budget goals and receive bonuses. For public agencies, the goal is to drive share value and/or pay dividends. In most cases, these cuts came at the expense of the producers and their families.

THE CORPORATE MODEL
(OR TRADITIONAL AGENCY MODEL)
THE WEEKLY SALES MEETING

Before joining IOA, the thing I dreaded most about the corporate agency I worked for was the weekly sales meeting. Our mandatory meeting was held Monday mornings, and every producer was obligated to attend, along with key account managers. We'd sit around a large table in the boardroom, and one by one we'd talk about what we did last week, whom we talked to, and what transpired. Then we shared our plans for the coming week. In other words, we were forced to meet each week to justify our existence.

I did fine during these meetings because I made a lot of calls and talked to a lot of people. It was easy to share what I was working on, but it was a total waste of time. I could've spent that time being productive, rather than discussing how productive I intended to be. That oversight didn't magically end at the close of the meeting either. My manager was always poking his head into my office every couple of days wanting to know what I was up to. If I was out of the office for any noticeable length of time, I had to be ready to spin some rosy sunshine about where I'd been and the awesome opportunities I'd been opening up.

Some salespeople need that, I think. They're not going to perform unless they're being monitored and micromanaged. But for people with a more entrepreneurial mindset like me, it was demeaning and had the opposite effect—it was demotivating.

MICROMANAGEMENT

Another producer and friend of mine, Nick, used to work for a big broker based in Florida. One day, he returned to his office unannounced and found a middle manager rummaging through his trash can. When he questioned her about it, she confessed she was just checking to make sure he didn't throw out any confidential information that should have been put in the shredder. Are you fricking kidding me? Someone in the ivory tower decided that it made sense to pay middle managers to do crap like this while only paying their producers 20 percent on a renewal? Brilliant!

OTHER MEETINGS

Managers just love to schedule meetings, don't they? Of course, they need to fill their day somehow and justify their own existence. Let's have a meeting to talk about a bunch of crap that could have been communicated by just sending a brief email. Am I right? Or, maybe we should all sit around and discuss what we found in everyone's garbage that should have gone into the shred bin. What a complete waste of time!

PRESSURE OF THE ANNUAL PRODUCTION GOAL

Let's face it, if you work in any kind of sales role, you're going to have a formal written goal, or at least you should have one. As a corporate producer, you will typically have an aggressive new business goal each year.

In large metropolitan areas like Los Angeles, New York, and Chicago, your goal might be $300,000 or $400,000 in new revenue. In smaller areas, it might be $50,000 or $100,000. Whatever your goal is, you'd better hit it in order to stay in good graces with management and stand the best chance of keeping your job. If you fall short, your employer can send you packing with nothing more than two weeks' notice and a pat on the back. Then, your clients will get reassigned to other producers, or they'll get turned into house accounts.

Even if you're a great performer year after year, many things could happen within a year to prevent you from hitting your goal: a family member could get sick, you could get sick or have some other personal issue come up, or you could simply just have an off year.

MERGERS AND ACQUISITIONS

There are a lot of things outside your control that could happen. For example, your boss could be terminated, and a new sales manager could be brought in—like what happened to Bruce Eades. Everything may have been going great for years until a change turns your world upside down.

If you think that's a long shot scenario, understand that there is a lot of merger and acquisition activity right now in the retail insurance industry, and there has been for several years. As I write this, USI Insurance Services has announced that it will purchase Wells Fargo Insurance Services USA, which is a huge merger. But this isn't just a phenomenon among Fortune 500 companies; it is also becoming more common with smaller companies as private equity firms continue buying up streams of income and paying crazy multiples. Agency owners who previously had no interest in selling are finding it hard not to sell when a lot of cash is being waved under their noses. An insurance agency has always been a reliable stream of income—and that's not going to change anytime soon. Agency owners will go for the payday when the timing and money is right.

As of the writing of this book, eight out of the top ten privately owned agencies are now controlled by private equity. At some point, these guys will demand a return on their investment, and the only place that can feasibly come from is reducing producer commissions or laying off staff.

As of early 2018, we're already starting to see layoffs at

some of these firms. Keep in mind, this is happening while economic times are very good. Can you imagine the bloodbath that will happen if things take a downward turn of any kind? As a producer, it just makes sense to be prepared. Once the ship starts sinking, it's usually too late.

One of my partners, James Baker, likes to quote Warren Buffet. He often says "Should you find yourself in a chronically leaking boat, energy devoted to changing vessels is likely to be more productive than energy devoted to patching leaks."

YOU DON'T OWN YOUR BOOK OF BUSINESS

What happens if your agency sells and you don't want to work for the new owner? Or what if you get terminated for missing your goal? Or maybe you just want to change firms or take a shot at starting your own agency. There's the issue of the non-compete or non-piracy agreement to deal with.

While the laws relating to these agreements vary from state to state, they are typically enforceable for two years, and they dictate that you can't take any of the agency's accounts with you. Some even go as far as to say you can't communicate with any prospect with whom you've had any contact during your employment with the prior agency. Even if you've had a strong and personal relationship with a client or prospect for ten or fifteen years, you can't sign them until the non-compete period is over. In other words, if you leave, you will have to start again from scratch and wait out the two-year period.

While it's probably easier to make a transition like this in your twenties or thirties, I know many producers who took the leap in their forties and fifties and became wildly successful. The bottom line is that it's more important than ever for every commercial producer to have a viable backup plan—a plan B—just in case the unthinkable ever happens.

THE INCOME CAP

Another pain point in the corporate model is that your earnings are capped. They may not be capped in writing, but they're capped from a practical standpoint, because there are only so many hours in a day and only so much one person can do.

When you're only getting paid 20 percent or 25 percent on your renewals, it's physically impossible to grow beyond a certain point unless you're writing very large accounts or have unlimited resources and a superstar support team at your disposal. For example, at a 20 percent renewal commission, your book would need to exceed $2 million in revenue to ever make more than $400,000. The fact is, most corporate producers have books that amount to less than $1 million, and they make less than $200,000 a year. You would have to write a lot of new business to see any significant change in your lifestyle.

At IOA, where the producers are compensated fairly with level commissions based on revenue, you earn $570,000 a year with a $1 million revenue book.

If you've managed to build a book of business and are making good money, in one fell swoop, your agency can change your contract—which happens all the time—and, it would set you back to square one. Just look what happened to Bruce and Sandy. It's probably happened to you or someone you know.

The corporate world is unstable and unpredictable, rife with factors that are simply out of your control. While the insurance industry displays a façade of granite buildings, fancy suits, and appearances of steadfastness and longevity, it's really a house of cards for the commercial producer.

IOA: A TURNKEY SOLUTION FOR STARTING YOUR OWN BUSINESS

Imagine having all the advantages and benefits of owning your own business without all the traditional headaches associated with running an agency. Now, further imagine having all the resources available at your fingertips that will enable you to compete and win on any account you work on. Would that get you fired up or inspired? Would you change your approach to the business in any way? How much more business do you think you would write?

When you own your own agency, you would naturally own every account that you write. You'd pay yourself as much as you could after paying your office expenses, and you could build a business with no size or income cap. That's essentially what we do at IOA, except that we're each building our own business within a larger corporate structure.

Unlike most local agencies, value-added resources are deployed by our in-house team versus being outsourced. When agencies outsource, delivery to the client can be unpredictable and inconsistent. There also is very little or no control of what these providers may be doing or how they may be advising your clients once they get "in there." Their interests may not always align with yours. At IOA, you will find the bench strength of our team to be consistent and strong. Your clients will benefit from the long-term relationships that stem from continuously receiving this kind of value over time.

In addition, you won't have to hire and train a staff, you won't have to establish procedural guidelines, you don't have to set up a bookkeeper or an accounting department, you won't need an HR department, and you won't have to run the vacuum or take out the trash. All you have to do is sell. Well, sell, keep your clients happy, and continue to grow your book. And, if you want to pitch in and act like a partner, you'll also be invited to purchase stock in the overall agency (in addition to the equity in your book).

Typically, producers who start their own agency can spend only a portion of their time selling because of all the other responsibilities that come with running a business (like hiring, firing, managing office drama, meeting with carriers, collecting receivables, etc.). There are a lot of headaches and hassles that accompany the freedom of entrepreneurship. As any agency owner will tell you, it's definitely not all glitz and glamor. I have several friends who have been successful at owning and running their own agencies. However, for every few who are super successful, there are dozens more who continuously struggle to attract markets, find and retain quality employees, and make ends meet.

Another beautiful thing about the IOA model, which the entrepreneur can appreciate, is if you ever decide to part ways, you can take your clients with you. You can set up your own shop or take your clients with you to your next job. Not only are you paid like an owner, you're treated like one.

Our CEO, Heath Ritenour, always says, "If you're not happy here, that's OK. You're free to leave and go where you'll be happy. And, we'll help you do it."

If you're performing well at your current company and earning a great income, it can be difficult to determine the right time to strike out on your own or make the transition to a company like IOA. This is the same dilemma anyone wanting to start a new business struggles with. You must first take a leap of faith, be confident in your ability, and have a plan to manage the transition financially. If you're not willing to invest in yourself, who else will invest in you?

IOA has been successful at helping with this transition to ensure a softer landing. In some cases, IOA has been able to help new producers buy their previous book of business (if their agency was willing to sell the book) by securing financing with its premium finance relationships. If an agency was not willing to sell the book, we've also provided a draw to help producers stay afloat and pay their bills while they're ramping up. Of course, any draw balance or other debt must be paid before the book can be moved.

When you become an owner, you take control of your future—I'm talking about complete control of your time, money, and relationships.

WHAT YOU NEED TO WORK AT IOA

This path isn't for everyone. If you're not a self-starter, you're not going to last long. It's just like beginning any kind of business—you have to be productive without a boss looking over your shoulder. You have to get up in the morning and hit the ground running. If you need a support staff to organize your time, set up your calls, make your coffee, or whatever else, you're probably better off sticking with your corporate gig.

Neither is this job for anyone unwilling or unable to take a financial risk. I went from making a guaranteed $75,000 to $80,000 a year to making zero, plus whatever I could drum up on my own in that first year. In order to limit my financial risk and keep stress to a minimum at a time when I needed to focus on building a business, I decided to drastically pare down my overhead. To that end, I was driving a $6,000 paid-off, reliable car and living in a small condo costing me about $400 a month. I understand it's not possible nor practical for everyone to skinny down their overhead to this extent, but I didn't want to take a draw or run up a bunch of debt.

It really just comes down to how bad you want it and what you're willing to sacrifice to make it happen. The company is extremely good about helping newcomers stay afloat, as I've mentioned, but if you're not ready to temporarily tighten the belt on the comfortable lifestyle you're accustomed to, then you should probably take a moment to reflect and examine your priorities—maybe you just prefer the status quo.

The bottom line is that you need to decide what you want for your future. Only you can make that choice. After all, it's your life and your dream!

At one time or another, I've asked most of my partners the same question, "Do you have any regrets about joining IOA, or would you do anything different if you had to do it all over again?" Invariably, they will say the same thing, "Only that I didn't do it sooner."

Chapter 1

===

PICTURING YOUR LIFE AT IOA

It's the annual awards dinner. You and 300 of the best producers from around the country fill a spectacular ball-room. In addition, there are suppliers and partners who contribute to sponsor the event and pay their gratitude. For IOA, this is our Academy Awards. If you've earned an award, the board of directors is onstage to welcome you when your name is called. Your picture is flashed up on the big screen for everyone to see. You shake everyone's hand and bask in the limelight and applause. It's heart-warming to be recognized by your peers, especially when there is no jealousy. Those not receiving awards are still striving and growing their books—knowing they, too, will be on that stage one day. They also understand that every producer on that stage is willing to lend a hand and help them get there.

We're here to recognize the best producers at three different levels of success. The first is $500,000 in revenue, and the award is a silver trophy of an eagle's head. The next level is $750,000 in revenue, represented by a golden trophy of an eagle's head. These are beautiful conversation pieces that look excellent in your office. And then there's the highest-level award: the presidential eagle trophy given to those who bring in $1 million in revenue or more. This bronze trophy is much larger than the other two, and it depicts the full body of an eagle flying with its wings spread wide.

My goal has been to add the presidential eagle trophy to the silver and gold trophies currently sitting on my shelves, and it's just now about to come true.

In 2016, thirty-eight producers (out of roughly 300) received the presidential eagle trophy. There's been a significant increase in the number of producers who've reached that benchmark over the last couple of years. Before that, fewer than two dozen did. And prior to that, only a handful. While that magic number might not be as rare as it used to be, it's still super special being able to achieve that level and share the stage with such an elite group of producers.

In fact, by the end of 2017, our company had almost fifty producers (out of 300) reach or exceed the $1 million revenue mark, which is amazing when you compare that with other agencies. In fact, we have a number of producers with books of business that exceed $2 million and some are in excess of $3 million. Those guys and gals are a rare breed of superstar, and it's awesome having the opportunity to work beside them and to learn from them.

INNOVATIONS THAT DISTINGUISH IOA AND THE ENTREPRENEURIAL MODEL

Because of our innovative approach to the traditional insurance industry, which I'll delve into below, IOA is growing rapidly.

OWNERSHIP

The primary reason it's called the Entrepreneurial Model is because you have true equity in your book of business. While some corporate agencies may offer token equity or shareholder status after a long period of paying your dues, at IOA, you have the chance to control your book from day one.

LEVEL COMMISSIONS

If you're like most producers, being paid 40 percent for new business and 20 percent on renewals (at best), you'll spend much of your time chasing prospects. To make any decent money, you'll need to write over $100,000 in new revenue every year, which means that's where you'll spend the bulk of your time. Your manager will also be keenly focused on where your time is spent. While you may love your existing clients and want to do right by them, in reality, servicing must fall more on the account manager's shoulders, which presents the risk of your clients feeling neglected when you're no longer as involved.

At IOA, renewal accounts are treated the same as new ones. You get the same commission split regardless of whether the business is new or a renewal. As a result, you're able (and are expected) to treat your existing clients with the attention and respect they deserve, which will naturally increase your retention rate and facilitate long-lasting relationships.

Personally, a long-term client is more valuable to me than a new one, so that's where I focus a lot of my time. Besides that, it takes a lot more time to acquire a new relationship than it does to cultivate an existing one. Don't get me wrong, I still love chasing new business and will usually write more of it every year than I ever did in the corporate model, but I will also frequently partner on new accounts to leverage my time. We only have so many hours in a day, and at IOA, I have the freedom to choose how I spend those hours, which is much more effective (instead of what's important to some schmo sales manager).

And because I have equity in my book of business, losing a client doesn't mean losing my employer's client—and a mere 20 percent commission. It means losing my own client. When talking to the owner of a business, I sometimes explain how we are in the same boat. Gaining a new client will increase my income and net worth, while losing a client reduces my income and net worth. It affects me just like it would the owner of any business. And as owners, we care more about what happens than any salesperson ever would.

THE NUMBERS

I touched on the numbers earlier. Let's take a closer look at the commission structure so if you're considering starting at IOA, you'll have some sense how much business you'll need to write to hit certain benchmarks.

The top commission split is 57 percent for both new business and renewals. This applies to a book of business at $750,000 or more. For books at $500,000, the split is 52 percent. Books north of $250,000, but less than $500,000 receive a 47 percent split, and below that, it is 42 percent, which typically is where you'll begin when you start. Even that lowest figure is more than double the industry average when you consider most agencies are only paying a 20 percent split on renewals. After five years, if your book has not grown to $250,000, you're probably not right for this kind of self-starting role and are probably better off at a corporate agency.

One thing that separates IOA from the rest of the industry is that while other companies look for ways to cut their producers' income by reducing commissions or raising the production bar, IOA is actively working to help its producers reach the highest possible commission split. Instead of a zero-sum game where the company wins at your expense or vice versa, IOA is set up where everyone can win.

NO SALES MANAGEMENT

In the Entrepreneurial Model, there is no manager looking over your shoulder. This built-in freedom can be a good or bad thing depending on whether you require a stick to motivate you, or you can provide your own motivation. For self-starters, the ability to be your own manager is a compelling reason to join IOA. We enjoy the ability to set our own schedules and structure our time in the way we deem best.

RELAXED ENVIRONMENT

Along those same lines, we offer producers the freedom to dress appropriately for their client and their geography, which might not necessarily involve a suit and tie. Living in Florida, many of us like to wear dress slacks and a nice golf shirt. Most clients are comfortable with this and dress in a similar fashion. I still maintain one nice suit in my closet for weddings, funerals, and the occasional formal presentation. I also have one nice sport coat, which I'm wearing in my author photo on the back cover of this book.

RESOURCES: WE DON'T PEDDLE POLICIES; WE BRING VALUE TO THE INSURANCE TRANSACTION

At IOA, you will have the resources to compete with the larger brokers, like HUB International, USI Insurance Services, Arthur J. Gallagher & Co., BB&T Insurance Services, Brown & Brown Insurance, etc. We have also won over clients from Marsh, Aon, and Willis. Whether it's finding a partner with the right expertise, using our proprietary RiskScore® system to improve your client's bottom line, leveraging our in-house claim advocates (licensed claim adjusters), mod analyst, HR Support, MyWave or LMS system, you will have the tools you need to compete on any account. While big brokers may offer a lot of sizzle with their fancy presentations, they frequently under deliver. At IOA, on the other hand, we lay out a service schedule on the calendar with checks in place to ensure our promises are monitored and kept. Our results speak for themselves; every month we share the new success stories via email for everyone in the company to celebrate.

Another benefit of working at IOA is that rather than competing against fellow producers for accounts (like some of our competitors), we're able to cooperate. We can share our skills, knowledge, and experience in order to be valuable resources for each other. This enables us to leverage our time and scale our businesses beyond what an individual producer can do on his or her own.

Here's an example. A while back, I stumbled upon a large specialty temp-staffing company, which had some nuanced insurance requirements that I wasn't familiar with. It was a large account, and I didn't want to walk away from the opportunity. So, I pulled in fellow partner, Rob Schild, who specializes in this niche. We teamed up, and while I met with the client in person, Rob attended via conference call. It was clear from the outset of the call that we were the experts, and the client's current broker had no clue what he was doing. We closed the deal right then and there on the phone. All I did was handle the initial paperwork, while Rob and his team handled the bulk of the service work on the account. We'll split the commission in half—28.5 percent for each of us—for as long as it's on the books. Not a bad deal, right?

The bottom line? With limited knowledge in this specialty niche, I was able to bring in an expert, improve the client's program, and create a win for all parties involved. The client was better off, my partner, Rob, wrote an account that he didn't have to prospect for, and I will receive payment into perpetuity for simply making the introduction, facilitating the process, and contributing as needed.

An even better example involved two of our larger producers, David Hendrick and Gary Smith. David insures an Orlando-based developer who recently partnered with a large international company to build a $76 million condo building near Central Park in New York City. To handle the insurance, the large company wanted to bring in their brokers, the New York City offices of Marsh and Aon. In addition, the general contractor also brought their broker (Brown & Brown) into the mix.

On the face, it would appear that David and Gary were at a disadvantage. They had to interview head-to-head against three behemoth brokers who would not only bring out their heavy artillery (polished expert team and presentations), but who also had strong relationships and a local presence in a completely different part of the country.

At the end of the day, Gary's expertise in putting together unique construction products (including large project specific policies) was huge as he worked with the client on some very detailed contract language and administrative recommendations. They were viewed as highly-trained professional advisors and ended up running circles around the competition. They landed the deal which generated about $280,000 in revenue.

While David had little expertise in this particular area, he was able to partner with Gary and create a huge win for everyone involved: the client, IOA, his partner, Gary, and himself. And over time, David will become a better producer because of the experience as his knowledge continues to grow.

With as many producers as we have—and continue to hire—you can always find someone with a particular expertise to help you out if need be. And, if you're willing to help others when you can, they are willing to help you.

In my opinion, it always pays to bring in an expert. Unless there is some kind of special relationship or politics in play, the expert will win over the generalist every time.

OPPORTUNITY TO LEVERAGE, SCALE, AND GROW THROUGH PARTNERING

Another benefit of cooperating with fellow producers is the ability to maximize your time, be more efficient, and leverage your income.

Let's return to the example of the temp-staffing account that I collaborated on earlier. I leveraged my effort and income through strategic partnering. Instead of committing to a lifetime of service on an account for a 57 percent level commission, I've enlisted a partner who will gladly carry most of the load while I receive half (or a 28.5 percent split) as long as the account remains on the books. My time is now free to work at the next opportunity. In theory, one could build his or her entire book of business like this at IOA.

Can you imagine having a $1 million-plus book of business with no direct client responsibility? What would your life look like? How would you spend your free time? Would you help others? I don't know of any producer currently taking it to this extreme and partnering on all of his or her accounts, but someone may take off and run with the idea after reading this. Or, maybe that person will be me!

When you are the only producer on an account, you (and your team) are 100 percent responsible for delivering service to that client. Because there are only so many hours in a day, you will eventually become a victim of your own success. Unless you find a way to leverage your efforts (through partnering, for example), you will eventually spend all your time servicing current clients with little time left to be proactive.

CARRIER QUOTAS

When I first started in the insurance business, I worked

for a small family agency that my dad owned. We had two regional insurance companies that were our primary carriers, and we had to spend our time focused on writing the business that *they* wanted to write. Each carrier had its own appetite, and we were forced to spend our time looking for those types of accounts. After all, we had to feed them, or they wouldn't be around for long. We also had to write enough business to be profitable, or they could cancel us for having a high-loss ratio. I recall being puckered up during some of those meetings, because we had most of our eggs in those two baskets, and we couldn't afford to get fired.

At IOA, we have about 300 producers, so we are able to feed our partner carriers and receive top-level recognition with many of them. You are completely free to pick and choose which financially-secure carriers you place business with and which types of accounts you want to write. Our underwriter relationships are also strong, because we honor our production commitments, and we don't waste their time (like some of our competitors who just block markets). For that reason, they usually look for ways to write business instead of finding excuses to decline.

Our top management is also engaged and maintains personal relationships with the senior management at all of our partner carriers. Our partner carriers also value the IOA relationship, because they understand we're the largest agency in the world that will never be up for sale. Since they know we aren't going anywhere, they're comfortable investing their time and resources in us knowing their efforts aren't being wasted.

STOCK OPTIONS

IOA has several subsidiaries, including a real estate holding company, a promotional products company, a payroll services company, an environmental wholesaler, a 401(k) advisor, a sports marketing company, a safety consulting firm, an information technology consulting firm, a printing and workflow consulting firm, and more. We also have a rapidly growing subsidiary that primarily acquires smaller insurance agencies. As producers, we are given the opportunity to buy shares of the overall company. Each subsidiary's results affect the overall performance of the stock available for purchase.

Each year, we're given the option to buy a certain number of shares, based on the size of our individual book of business. The larger your book, the more shares you have the option to purchase.

IOA's stock has performed well since 1988, significantly outpacing the stock market. I personally know the people who are running and growing the sub-companies, so I have a high comfort level buying this stock rather than some publicly traded stocks I know little about. While no one can predict returns will be like in the future, I'm extremely confident in our team.

In addition, we have the chance to contribute to the success of the sub-companies by referring business to them during the year. We even have a friendly internal competition every year to see how many referrals we can send them. While I've personally sent many referrals, I've also received many referrals in return. We are all in this together helping each other grow and get better.

DOES IOA OFFER A 401(K) FOR PRODUCERS?

No. At IOA, most producers are compensated by 1099 and have established our own LLC or Subchapter S Corp. We don't qualify to participate in the IOA 401(k) plan.

While I understand the thought of losing your corporate 401(k) might seem scary at first, the good news is that this is your money, and you can usually take it with you. Personally, I believe we've all been brainwashed into thinking our 401(k) is the best way of saving for retirement. If you haven't done so, please read the best-selling book, *The Power of Zero* by David McKnight; you will never look at your 401(k) the same.

If you still want a 401(k), you can start a more flexible one through your LLC or S Corp. Personally, I prefer the Solo 401(k) where you can contribute much more than you can under a corporate plan (up to $61,000 per year in 2018). These can be set up in the traditional tax-deferred way or as a Roth. With a Solo 401(k), you can also invest in nontraditional things, such as real estate, land, mortgages, deeds, private loans, tax liens, private businesses, gold, stocks, bonds, mutual funds, and even cryptocurrency.

At IOA, our Private Client Group can also show you how to set up an indexed universal life (IUL) policy and how to legally overfund it for additional tax-free income at retirement. This is a great way to protect your family in the event of your premature death or a long-term care stay. This little-known strategy is extremely powerful and is described in detail by Patrick Kelly in his best-selling book, *The Retirement Miracle.*

Keep in mind, the Solo 401(k) and IUL are entirely optional and will be in addition to the equity you accumulate in your book of business along with any IOA stock you opt to purchase, plus the value of any other investments you choose to make from your additional earnings. Since you will be earning two or three times what you were before, take a moment to do some math. How much better will your retirement be? How much more can you accumulate?

If you have at least ten years left before retirement, the

difference can be in the millions—or sooner if you happen to be a great producer, a great investor, or live in a state like California, where you may be able to move your book at any time without the encumbrance of a non-compete agreement.

BUILT-IN PERPETUATION

When the day comes for you to eventually retire, or God forbid you should prematurely pass away or become disabled, our contract provides for IOA to purchase your book of business for up to two times its annual revenue based on tenure. This is paid out to you or your heirs over a six-year period. Ideally, you will select a specific producer or producers you wish to pass your business on to and start working closely with them within five years of your anticipated retirement. This will ensure a seamless transition and best possible result. If your successors are able to grow your book of business, you can actually receive more than two times.

If done correctly, the right successor(s) will create a win for everyone involved, including the producer, the company and, most importantly, the client (who benefits from a stress-free transition). To that end, IOA has implemented a formalized mentor/mentee program that provides a platform to help you accomplish this. More details on this program will follow later in the book.

A COMPANY FOR THE GENERATIONS

As mentioned by John Ritenour (our founder and chairman) earlier, he wanted to make sure the company would be generational, meaning it would never be for sale, never go public, never merge, etc. He wanted the company to be here for generations to come so you could build your business without worrying about the dreaded "company announcement" coming down one day and rocking your world. You can plan for the future and pass your business down to your child or anyone else of your choosing. Our CEO, Heath Ritenour, has reiterated this on numerous occasions, but I think it's important enough to bear repeating: "IOA is not for sale and will never be for sale. When anyone asks, my answer is not only no, but hell no!"

DECENTRALIZED MANAGEMENT

To address our rapid expansion, we've also adapted our management structure. We've divided up the country into five regions and tapped highly qualified producers to manage each respective region and serve on the board. Prior to establishing these regions, our CEO and president (Heath Ritenour and Jeff Lagos) were involved in almost every decision.

The regional presidents—also full-time producers—are now empowered to make most decisions, as they have a much better understanding of the nuances of their particular geographic area. As a result, we're an extremely flat company in terms of hierarchy. There are no layers of middle management or bureaucracy, which makes us nimble and quick to respond to any issue that might arise.

ATTRACTIVE TO MILLENNIALS

The younger generation hasn't shown much interest in the insurance business. A recent survey indicated that just 4 percent of millennials thought favorably of insurance as a career choice. I get it; it's not as cool as being a tech entrepreneur, but one of the things that makes IOA more lucrative to young people is that our structure is geared to entrepreneurial types, offering more risk/reward than employment in the corporate world.

Another factor that makes us a lucrative alternative is the work-life balance that we offer, which young people value. They also want to work for causes they believe in; they're not just interested in money.

If you're a millennial reading this book, I encourage you to consider the power of earning residual income, also known as "level renewal" commissions. Compare this compensation plan with other traditional professions like law, medicine, or public accounting where you're required to work crazy hours for many years in order to make good money. As a successful insurance producer, you can make as much (or more) than a partner in any of those industries. In addition—and maybe even more importantly—your quality of life is better with less stress and more time for yourself, family, hobbies, interests, and so on. If you have what it takes and are a self-starter, you could pay those student loans off sooner, not to mention buying big items like a car or house. Best of all, you won't need a side hustle or have to change careers and reinvent yourself every few years—not unless you just want to.

COMMUNITY SERVICE

We're supportive of the communities we're in, and we're frequently opening new offices in new locations all over the map. We support a lot of organizations within the communities we work in. There's a list of thirty or more on our website, which is just a drop in the bucket. Because servant leadership is part of the fabric of our culture, it's understood that we're going to be involved in supporting and serving our communities.

MY EXPERIENCE AT IOA

I was thirty-seven years old when I left the agency I was with to join IOA. I had a goal of $50,000 in annual business then, which was being adjusted to $100,000. I'm fifty-four now and am just reaching my personal goal of having a $1 million plus revenue book. Can't wait to have that bronze eagle trophy in my office!

Each year, I make about three times more than I would with any other big broker, and I have complete freedom and flexibility.

I've put together a growing nest egg that would've been impossible had I stayed at that local agency or even if I'd joined one of the majors. I've also had the pleasure of spending time with my family and serving my community. I've been able to do it my way.

It was, without a doubt, the right choice for me. It was the right choice for a diverse group of others I know too. Whether it's the right choice for you is the subject of the next chapter.

Chapter 2

IS IOA RIGHT FOR YOU?

There have been loads of successful producer transitions to IOA. Allow me to share some of them. Maybe you will be next!

DAVID HENDRICK

You've already heard me mention David before. To me, his story is probably the most unlikely, and it's also one of the most inspiring.

After getting his license and applying for producer positions at several agencies (without success) in late 2001, David landed a job working as an underwriting assistant with a major insurance carrier. He figured he could get some good experience and maybe transition to the agency side and become a producer after about ten years. After being on the job only about a month, the devastating events of September 11, 2001, rocked the country and changed the insurance carrier's outlook abruptly. It wasn't long before 10 percent of the staff—about 25,000 employees—were being laid off. Rather than sit around and wait for the inevitable, David reached out to his mom, who was a successful producer at IOA, and said, "Hey, I don't care if I'm emptying the garbage or licking stamps, can you get me an entry-level position at IOA?"

His mother, Beth Hendrick, and Rick Dalrymple (both successful IOA producers) stepped up and handed off some of their smaller accounts to help David. His initial book was only about $30,000 in total revenue, but David was ecstatic. That was all the incentive he needed to roll up his sleeves and get to work.

Being introverted, David was actually afraid to call his own clients in the beginning. He reasoned they would be disappointed and that he would be a huge downgrade compared to the agents they had been used to working with. However, on the upside, he was able to devote more time to assisting and problem solving for them. His confidence grew with time and maturity.

While the words introvert and successful producer aren't usually found in the same sentence, David discovered by experience that he had a knack for cold calling. While you will never catch him at a rubber chicken dinner or networking event, he has no qualms whatsoever about being rejected over the phone. He started out by making 125 cold calls per week to open conversations and get new clients on board, but then he would weld the door shut behind him by providing stellar service, attention to detail, and getting things done for people. It didn't take long for him to land a few large accounts, and he hasn't looked back since.

Today, David's book is over $1 million in revenue and growing. He credits his awesome service team along with partnering with other producers for his success. Today, he partners on at least 80 percent of his accounts. He insures over 120 condo associations along with accounts in the hospitality and construction space. He is frequently sought out by other producers to be the go-to partner on new deals. Yes, David has come a long way since those meager beginnings, and he continues to be grateful every day for the opportunity.

And, yes, he still likes to make those cold calls!

ALI POOL

Ali Pool was a successful producer with one of the big brokers for about thirteen years. She had built a large book and was pulling down a nice, comfortable income. She had always met her goals, was pretty happy with her situation, was doing well, and was not looking to make a change. And really, why would she want to? How many people do you know willing to take a risk and walk away from that type of situation?

It was actually her husband who first suggested she consider giving IOA a shot. He (along with Ali) had become friends with several IOA producers on some of the insurance company trips and had gotten to understand more about the entrepreneurial model and the potential upside. Ali said, "Do you realize, this isn't a real good idea? That's a lot of money we're walking away from!" But her husband is a numbers guy and said, "Yeah, but at IOA, you'll be back to what you're making in a couple of years, and you'll own it." They looked at it as an investment and reasoned that *you need to do something different if you want to have something different.*

Ali also kicked the tires at a few other local agencies before deciding on IOA. The lack of carriers and resources at those smaller agencies was a drawback for her. At the large agency, she had enjoyed having the guns (and insurance carriers) to go after big accounts. She liked the idea of IOA having so many producers contributing to all the carrier goals. She also liked the many solid relationships in place. When a fellow producer—and someone she really looked up to—made the decision to join IOA, it got her attention. "My goodness," she thought. "One of our absolute best producers just left to go with IOA. I'm going too."

Ali recalls her first year being challenging because her non-compete wouldn't permit her to work on or even call anyone she had ever worked with at that big agency. She basically started from scratch.

Despite starting from zero, Ali managed to book about $200,000 in revenue within her first two years. Now, five years later, she has seventy accounts with about $750,000 in total revenue. Her income this year will be more than double what it was at the old agency. She also enjoys having freedom and flexibility to spend more time on her accounts. In addition, she now owns a substantial asset (her book equity) and has complete control of her time and future.

Her ultimate goal is to have less than one hundred accounts that bring in $1 million plus in revenue. She's closing in on this goal and readily acknowledges it wouldn't have been possible without the IOA opportunity—for which she is extremely grateful.

She also gives a lot of credit for her success to Jeremy Burr, a successful IOA producer who provided mentoring early on and who also teaches the annual IOA Sales Academy (which we will discuss later in the book). Ali attended his classes and said, "I would call him, and he was so patient. He gave me so many different ideas that I just said, 'You know what, this guy knows what he's doing, and I'm going to do everything he tells me to do!' I owe a lot of my success at IOA to Jeremy, for sure!"

BRUCE EADES

You may recall Bruce's story from the introduction. He joined IOA (along with a few other producers) after his employer announced a commission cut, took away accounts, and brought in a tyrant for a sales manager who essentially stole their freedom.

Before joining IOA, Bruce and the others explored several options, including buying an agency. After a few meetings with IOA's founders, John and Valli Ritenour, however, Bruce said, "The Lord gave us peace, and we knew IOA was the right move."

Bruce (and the other producers working with him at the time) was also able to negotiate the purchase of some accounts. As Bruce recalls, "It was like going through a divorce. It was rough. We had less than five days to come up with half a million dollars or the deal was off." At the time, John stepped up and sent the check. It was done on a handshake and a mutual trust they had developed with each other in those first few meetings. This was a lifesaver, as it provided Bruce and the others with a soft landing at IOA, along with additional time to come up with a plan to pay back the money. After six months, they repaid the loan, plus interest. After a few weeks, because of Bruce's extraordinary commitment to IOA, John sent all the interest back. That's just the kind of person he is.

After joining IOA with a fairly small book of business, Bruce chose to become a niche specialist and has become wildly successful. Today, he runs a Managing General Underwriter within IOA called USA Telecom Insurance Services. With Nationwide Insurance as their lead carrier, they offer the only admitted program in the United States for cell tower contractors. According to Bruce, "Niching has been good to me—*extremely* good. They say if you niche, you get rich. There is a lot of truth to that." He believes in focusing on an odd niche, not a dry cleaner program or something everyone else is chasing after. He has also become proficient with LinkedIn and has developed a strategy that works fantastically for generating leads and clients.

Today, Bruce serves as a regional president of IOA. He is still based in Gainesville, Georgia, and has a book of business well in excess of $1 million in revenue.

When talking to prospective new producers, Bruce is always happy to share his experience:

"The beautiful part about IOA is that it's the best contract in the industry. Not only do you have equity in your book, you also have the richest commission structure in the world. And think about this, most people would be happy with a low commission split if they had equity. Other people would be happy with a high commission split with no ownership and no equity. At IOA, we have both. To double down even more, if you act like a partner, you are invited to be a stockholder on top of that. And the fourth leg is the amazing sales culture we have. Anybody in this organization will help anybody else, so our culture is awesome!"

Bruce also believes in our responsibility to give back and wants to share this takeaway:

"We have been given such an unbelievable opportunity, and sometimes we lose sight of that as producers. When John Ritenour created this company, he made the decision to give back. Not only does he give back in his personal life and give back to causes that are important to him, he's also created rich deals for us. What I think is not communicated enough is that we have an awesome responsibility to give back to whatever causes or charities we're passionate about. I believe, if we do that, we will continue to be blessed not only as a company, but as producers."

ROSS EVANS

Bruce Eades has also taken time to mentor his nephew, Ross Evans. Ross is twenty-six years old and has been selling insurance for only a few years. I'm always intrigued when talking with a new producer who's had success early on. For one, it took me a lot longer to get there, and I enjoy learning about how they're doing it. And secondly, you don't see very many young people or millennials flocking to the insurance business these days, so I always like to hear why and how they ended up with a career in insurance.

For Ross, the idea wasn't unusual at all. His uncle had been telling him since he was twelve years old that he'd be good at the insurance business, but at the time, Ross was more interested in sports. He played several sports in high school and even played some soccer at the college level in Maryland for a few years. He eventually decided soccer wasn't the best use of his time and transferred to the University of Georgia, earning a degree from their risk management and insurance program.

While Ross had envisioned starting out as a retail producer after graduation, the wholesalers were offering a better salary. In the short run, it was great. They offered him a $50,000 salary along with benefits, which was pretty good considering his cost of living at the time was low. He also found he was talented at being a wholesaler. He understood coverage better than most of the retail producers, and he could talk circles around them when it came to explaining why their clients needed it.

When they rolled out his incentive plan, Ross did some quick math in his head. "In order to go from making $50,000 to $100,000, I've got to write over $9 million in premium." Although aggressive and young, he realized the wholesale side wasn't the best fit for him. What's more, he knew he could be making more than $500,000 if he wrote that same amount of premium working with Uncle Bruce at IOA. And to top everything off, he wasn't too thrilled about the wholesale lifestyle where he was pretty much chained to his desk, churning and burning a lot of phone calls and not traveling outside of the office very much.

After about a year with the wholesaler, Ross decided to join IOA. He wanted to own his own business and determine his own success. He wanted to have control over his future, and he loved the idea of being able to out-earn the CEO. None of those were possible on the wholesale side. He also understood the best time to do it was while he had little overhead and his largest responsibility was feeding his dog (as opposed to waiting ten more years when he'd likely have huge responsibilities—like a wife, children, mortgage, and the whole nine yards).

Since that fateful day he decided to bet on himself, Ross

has never looked back. He started making a bunch of cold calls right out of the gate, which landed him two large farm accounts (by partnering with two agriculture experts, Terry Crawford and Cole Hubka, in our South Florida office). This early success provided a huge boost, and he's been building upon that base ever since. In addition to leveraging the partnership opportunities, Ross has also taken advantage of the many other tools at IOA for bringing value to his clients, including RiskScore,® Risk Services, POA (payroll processing), and so on.

After two years at IOA, Ross is twenty-six years old with a book of business close to $250,000 in annual revenue with a net worth around half a million dollars. He's also noticed that newer producers are starting to bring him in as the senior guy to partner on some deals. He eclipsed the $100,000 income mark and is barely getting started. He sees many young producers at other agencies and thinks to himself, "Man, they're really missing the boat! They're over there churning and burning for corporate stock when they could be making double or triple and building some real wealth."

Ross also wants to help spread the word to other young people who may have found success in other industries, but without control of their future. He frequently tells others, "Imagine putting the same kind of effort into something where you get rewarded for every minute of time spent and every ounce of effort you throw into it! Why not own your own success? If you're the type of person who's going to be working hard anyway, why not work where you get rewarded for it? Especially if you're going to be there for roughly two-thirds of your waking life. Let's do this thing!"

COLE HUBKA AND TERRY CRAWFORD

Cole Hubka joined a leading IOA competitor as a producer after graduating college in 2003. In his first five years, he experienced a lot of success. The economy was good, and construction was exploding. It seemed like an easy job to him—really easy. At the time, landscapers were paying $250,000 in premium, and every condo association was paying extremely inflated pricing, so he wrote lots of contractors, landscapers, and condos. By the fifth year, his book of business was generating roughly $800,000 in total revenue. That's when he learned about the IOA opportunity.

Before joining IOA, Cole looked into some other agencies, but the IOA contract was so strong (with the high-level commission split and equity), it seemed ridiculous not to do it. Cole's dad is an attorney. He also reviewed the IOA contract and loved it. For Cole, it was like an opportunity to make professional sports-level money. So, he decided to take a shot and go for it. He was twenty-seven years old at the time and figured he'd probably be retired by age thirty-five.

He was also able to purchase three of his large construction accounts, which would provide a base income while he was getting cranked up. Then, the unthinkable happened. The Great Recession hit, and construction came to a screeching halt. Two of the accounts he had purchased went out of business. The third dropped in size substantially, leaving Cole about $70,000 in-the-hole right out of the gate. Talk about a shocker. It's hard to imagine a tougher scenario for a young producer to be faced with. While this could have been an opportunity to get depressed or down, that never crossed Cole's mind. He's never been one to sit back.

With construction and the economy in the tank, Cole was ready to switch gears and started exploring alternate ways to rebuild his book and dig out of the hole. It was about that time that veteran producer, Terry Crawford, popped his head into Cole's office and offered to partner up and teach him the agricultural (Ag) business—a niche where IOA had a competitive advantage in the marketplace. At the time, Terry had a large book of Ag business and was approaching the later stages of his career. Terry liked the idea that Cole looked a "little younger" than him. He also liked the idea of working together to build up the agribusiness division within IOA. It was great timing for

Cole, as he could learn about a unique industry and benefit from all of Terry's specialized knowledge and expertise.

Once they hit the ground running, they've never looked back. Cole and Terry have been successful building this niche and growing their books and the division every year since first teaming up in 2010. Neither shows any sign of slowing down, either! They are both making money and having fun. And when Terry eventually decides to slow down and retire, his perpetuation plan with Cole is already in place.

While it took Cole a few more years than expected to ramp up due to the initial setbacks, he still says he wouldn't change a thing. He said, "The quality of life is just so much better here. There's enough anxiety in the insurance business already, so it's nice to know you have a good place to work where people care about you. And it's great to know they won't kick you out the door if you happen to struggle for a year or two. The flexibility has also been great now that I have a child. When you can control your time and money, a lot of things are possible. And you have all the resources you would ever need. If you're not successful here, then you've got to look in the mirror. This probably isn't the place for you."

Terry also agrees with Cole. He says having control of your time and money is huge. When asked if he had any regrets about joining IOA, Terry says his only regret is not doing it sooner.

MANY DIFFERENT PERSONALITIES

As you can see from these few stories, producers who succeed at IOA come with many different personality types and from a variety of backgrounds. It doesn't matter whether you're male or female, young or old, or whether you are a niche player or a generalist. There is no particular personality type or stereotype that works better than another. You can also be successful starting in your twenties or starting in your fifties. Personally, I would certainly recommend joining sooner rather than later.

It also doesn't hurt to be a highly motivated self-starter with a strong work ethic and an intense, consistent focus.

ATTRIBUTES NECESSARY TO THRIVE

Some people are naturally successful at whatever they do. They might have a gift, or perhaps they're wired a specific way. Those kinds of people find success anywhere, but for most of us, we have to put in the work to be successful and working at IOA is no different. As I've previously mentioned, IOA is not for everyone. Certain attributes are necessary in order to thrive.

DRIVE

In order to be successful at IOA, you must be a self-starter and have the drive to work hard, put in the hours, and grind it out. If you aren't motivated to grow your book, it's not worth it, and you're probably better suited for a corporate environment. If you're somebody who needs a manager to look over your shoulder and give you things to do, IOA is not the environment for you.

There's a perceived comfort zone when you work in a corporate environment. I say perceived because at any given time, they could cut your commission for no apparent reason. Or worse, they could fire you if they just don't like you anymore. It happens all the time. As an employee of a corporation, your job and livelihood are at the mercy of board members, CEOs, and managers. Board members often mandate changes in order to drive more profit to the bottom line, and sometimes those decisions don't consider the producers and how they might be affected. At IOA, on the other hand, our board of directors knows exactly how any changes will affect producers because they will affect them just the same. As I mentioned before, most of our board members are also producers.

SEE THE BIG PICTURE

You must be able to see the big picture and yet bite off one piece at a time. It's OK to hit singles and doubles, and build your business brick by brick, but you will also want to use your drive and resources to pursue some larger accounts and opportunities. After all, there's a lot to be said for diversification. This is not only a good idea with your personal investments, but also with your book of business.

Some of our producers just prefer to elephant hunt or write large accounts. For example, one guy in our office only had five accounts. I had over one hundred accounts at the time, but our books were similar in revenue size. He was hitting home runs while I was hitting singles and doubles. Although there are no hard-and-fast rules on how you run your business (you're free to do it however you'd like!), my book was obviously more diversified. If I lost an account, I wouldn't lose any sleep. If he lost an account, however, he'd lose 20 percent of his income overnight (yikes!).

The beauty of working as an IOA producer though is you can match your book of business to your personality and build it out any way you want.

DISCIPLINE

Another important attribute for success is discipline. Since you don't report to a manager or a boss, when you get out of bed every day, you have the option of lazing about and watching *Sports Center* or gearing up for a full day of work.

You have to structure your day in order to get the results you want to get, whatever that means for you. Perhaps that means one day is set for prospecting, the next day is for organization and paperwork, and the following day for follow-up calls and face-to-face visits. No one will organize your days for you at IOA; that responsibility is yours and yours alone. For me, this is where you find your freedom and independence, and it's another example of how you can tailor your business to fit your own personality and what works best for you.

TIME MANAGEMENT

In addition to discipline, time management is hugely important. Just like you need discipline to structure your work, you have to manage your time accordingly. It's easy to lose track of time with distractions like the internet, your phone, the TV, and even other producers. You have to be disciplined enough to create your structure in a way where you are using time to your advantage—and that will mean different things to everyone.

DETERMINING IF YOU'RE A GOOD FIT

Not sure if IOA is right for you? I've compiled some advice for you to determine if you're a good fit.

EXAMINE YOUR CURRENT SITUATION

First and foremost, examine how your current career translates to working as a producer for IOA. What does your current job look like day to day? What do you do? A lot of times, we've had a successful producer make the switch and say, "I do the same thing as I did at my previous agency. I'm just doing it here and I own my book of business." If you're successful working in a corporate environment, there's no reason you can't be successful at IOA. If you've built a strong network of people who refer you opportunities (like influencers or strategic partners such as attorneys or CPAs), or if you're active in your local Rotary Club or the community, none of that will change if you change employers, because all of that is transferable.

If you possess all the qualities we mentioned earlier in the chapter, IOA is likely a fit for you. If you set your own schedule and are already disciplined, you're not going to all of a sudden lose these attributes. If you've built your business right, you can continue doing so with IOA. You don't need the crutch of a public company to maintain your success. When you meet with clients, the only thing outwardly different is your business card.

OTHER INDUSTRIES

Just because you might work in an unrelated industry, doesn't mean your skills won't transfer to selling insurance. One of the most successful insurance producers I've seen sold construction materials to contractors before making the jump to selling insurance. With his vast network and through the relationships he'd built in construction, selling insurance translated fairly well for him. He was able to build a large book of business through his contacts, even in a different and unrelated field. His interpersonal relationships and time-management skills suited him well. It's not always essential to have insurance-specific experience to be successful with us.

PEO AND PAYROLL REPRESENTATIVES

Professional Employer Organizations (PEOs) and payroll representatives tend to make great referral partners and can also make excellent producers. They're used to actively prospecting and establishing relationships with a lot of the same people who are good for insurance. They make similar pitches and often deal with the same decision makers (owners, CFOs, or HR managers). In addition to transferable skills, PEO and payroll reps are typically well versed in HR, payroll, and tax-related issues. They can uncover areas of pain with a prospect that a Property & Casualty (P&C) or benefits producer may not be able to.

I've had some mutually beneficial referral partnerships with outside PEO and payroll reps for many years. While they are not part of IOA, they will walk me in with a favorable introduction. These are typically prospects experiencing some kind of pain, and we tend to close a high percentage of them. If you're a PEO or payroll rep, you may be a perfect fit for IOA, because you're already doing several aspects of the job. Or, if you're happy working on the PEO or payroll side, let's talk about how we can both benefit from a strategic partnership.

MENTOR PROGRAM

We also have a mentor program where younger people with little or no prior insurance experience can learn by working side by side with a veteran producer. More details on this will follow in a later chapter.

Chapter 3

═══

SETTING YOURSELF UP FOR SUCCESS

TRANSITIONING FROM THE CORPORATE MODEL TO IOA

In hindsight, the corporate model seemed stable to me at the time. I was a reliable producer and received a steady paycheck from a pretty large company. My check showed up every two weeks on the dot—I didn't have to wonder if it was coming. I also received a bonus on a quarterly basis when my production exceeded my base salary. As I mentioned before, it was a quality agency with a great group of people. All in all, it wasn't bad.

It also seemed stable because they paid for my health

insurance, and I had an auto allowance of $600 per month, which was a stellar car payment two decades ago. The company also offered a 401(k) with an employer matching contribution at up to 5 percent of my pay.

As I mentioned before, it was comfortable, but I was lacking inspiration. I was going through the motions and essentially playing it safe. It just wasn't the independent, robust life I really wanted.

I also figured that (worst case) I could easily get another comfortable corporate gig if it didn't work out. So with little to lose and so much to gain, I said, "Let's do this!" But before strutting my newly enlightened independent self into the boss's office to resign, there were some things to be done. I needed a plan, and, you should have a plan too.

SEEK COUNSEL AND UNDERSTAND WHAT YOU'VE SIGNED

Before doing anything, you'll want to meet with an attorney to, at the very least, review your non-compete agreement thoroughly and make sure you understand exactly what you can and can't do. It's going to vary by state, and it's going to vary by agreement. Some will be more restrictive than others.

Some recruiters or headhunters will tell you, "Go ahead

and violate your agreement and let them sue you." Or an agency will hire you and say, "Switch all your accounts over, and we'll support you when the lawsuit comes in. When they sue you, the worst thing that can happen is that you'll just have to pay for the accounts—which is really all you wanted in the first place." And that *is* one way to do it if your former agency won't sell you your business.

We don't operate that way at IOA; everything is above-board. We want to honor our agreements and do things the right way. We won't get involved in anything like that, but we do have two, great in-house attorneys who routinely look at these agreements. If there's any question about what you're allowed to do, they can assist with an interpretation. Nobody wants to get involved in a lawsuit. They're nasty things and can be easily avoided.

My non-compete was pretty straightforward. Like most, it was essentially a non-piracy agreement saying that I couldn't take any of the agency's accounts for two years. That's about all that's enforceable in most states. In California, these agreements generally aren't enforceable, so a producer may be free to accept business from his or her accounts, provided no confidential information is used in the process. That's one reason California has become our fastest-growing state and will likely surpass Florida to become our largest presence in the near future.

BOOK OF BUSINESS

After understanding my non-compete, the next step in my plan was to try and purchase my book of business. I thought it was a long shot. I also knew that I'd better be prepared for them to say no the moment I raised the question, because after that there would be no turning back. In fact, they could easily just ask me to pack my desk right on the spot.

When I entered the boss's office to announce my resignation, I also spewed my well-rehearsed speech about how great my client relationships were and explained how there was no possible way they would retain my clients after I left. I suggested that they might as well go ahead and sell them to me and get some value for them, rather than run the risk of ending up with squat. It was a convincing argument, or so I thought. You know what he said? At first, my boss asked if there was any chance I would reconsider my decision. When I said no, he wasted little time in wishing me the best of luck and also letting me know they would be keeping my accounts. I said, "Are you sure?" He said with a grin (in his best imitation from the old hit TV show, *Who Wants to be a Millionaire)*, "Yep, and that's my final answer!" After the reality eventually sunk in, I was a little bummed, but in hindsight, his answer was actually pretty funny.

If you're successful in getting your agency to sell your book, they will likely insist on payment up front. While your relationship may have been great up to this point, you're now viewed as an outsider, and they probably won't trust you to make payments over time. If you don't have the cash, IOA may be able to help. Most producers don't have that kind of money lying around, and it's generally not optimal to tap into your 401(k). At IOA, we have numerous finance company relationships that can assist. Most producers find that a low-interest loan payable over five years works pretty well.

Because of the larger commission split you get at IOA (you'll be making at least double), you can generally make the loan payments while still enjoying about the same income stream you were making before. And once the loan is paid, you'll be making twice as much.

PAST IS PROLOGUE

The past is usually a pretty good predictor of the future. If other producers have left your agency and the agency has been willing to sell a book of business, chances are they'll be willing to sell you your book too. If they've told other producers to pound sand and they keep their book, then that's likely what's going to happen when you ask.

One thing you can do to persuade them, though, is to share the statistic where 70 percent of your book of business won't be there after two years anyway. And after two years, you're going to take whatever's left because you'll still have those relationships. Since they're going to lose most of it anyway, they may as well just go ahead and sell you the whole thing and receive full value for it. Maybe you'll have more luck with this than I did.

In most cases, it's more valuable for them to sell it to you. However, don't be surprised if they're afraid of setting a precedent. I mean, what agency owner wants all their producers lining up and saying, "I'm going to IOA. Now sell me my book."

BUSINESS PLAN

Since buying my book was no longer an option, I needed to create a plan. Because LinkedIn and Facebook hadn't been invented yet and not everyone was using email at the time, my initial plan was pretty basic and revolved around generating as much activity as possible, including networking and making a set number of calls each day. I wasn't very good on the phone, so I spent what little I could afford on a professional appointment setting service, which supplemented the appointments I was able to make on my own. Bottom line, my plan was to grind it out, stay focused, and make some intelligent progress in the direction of my goal every day. If I did that, I knew I would eventually get there and become successful.

Whether or not you can buy your book, you will still want to have a written business plan. Even if it's fairly simple, it's essential to write it down so you have a road map of where you want to go. You can also refer to it periodically to ensure you're on track and continuously making progress in the right direction.

NEED SOME HELP WITH YOUR PLAN?

Lucky for you, times have changed, and great resources are now available everywhere to assist with your planning.

The best planning tool I've ever seen for insurance producers is included in an e-book published by IOA-sponsored Inforum called *The Unbound Producer*. It provides a detailed checklist where you can compare all the components of your current job to what you will receive in the Entrepreneurial Model (including compensation), so you'll know exactly what to expect. The chart has been reprinted below with their permission.

JOB COMPONENT	CURRENT MODEL	ENTREPRENEUR MODEL	DIFFERENCE
Commissions – New What percentage is paid and what is the difference from your current compensation. How much pressure is there to focus heavily on new business versus renewal of accounts.	40% x $100,000 20% of Total Book	52% x $100,000 20% of Total Book	$12,000/yr.
Commissions – Renewal What percentage is paid and what is the difference from your current compensation. What is the typical balance of new accounts versus renewals?	20% x $400,000 80% of Total Book	52% x $400,000 80% of Total Book	$128,000/yr.
Equity Ownership Is there opportunity for equity ownership? If yes, how long does it take to build this up.	None	✓ > 5 years	
Stockholder Options Is there an opportunity to own stock in the company? If so, when is this option available.	None	✓ > $250k	
Access to Markets Does the company have access to highly rated markets? If so, how many?	✓ 35	✓ 35	Same
Health Insurance Does the company offer a robust health insurance plan?	✓	✓	
Payroll Support Does the company offer support for handling all payroll details?	✓	✓	

JOB COMPONENT	CURRENT MODEL	ENTREPRENEUR MODEL	DIFFERENCE
Accounting/Tech Support Does the company offer support for account and technology?	✓	✓	
Claims Advocate Support Does your company provide support for your clients when they have a claim?	✓	✓	
Proprietary Tools Does your company provide Fortune 500 quality tools for customer aid and retention?	✓	✓	
Office/Desk Space Rental Is office/desk space part of your package, or must this be rented?	✓	✓	
Account Executive/Office Staff Are you provided with a quality staff support team?	✓	✓	
Office Expenses/Utilities Are your offices expenses covered?	✓	✓	
Licensing Does your company take care of management and fees for ongoing licensing?	✓	✓	
Marketing Are marketing expenditures provided by the company?	✓	✓	
Car/Travel Expenses Are you reimbursed for auto and other travel expenditures?	✓	✓	

JOB COMPONENT	CURRENT MODEL	ENTREPRENEUR MODEL	DIFFERENCE
Computer/Technology Hardware Does your company provide up-to-date technology, or does your company tend to lag behind or allow too long of a gap in upgrades?	✓ *Fairly current tech*	✓ *Fairly current tech*	
Ownership/Corporate Values Do the values of the company's leadership align with your own?	✓	✓	
Leadership Transparency Does your company leadership share openly about the decisions, direction, and financial health of the organization?	✓	✓	
Leadership Oversight Style Do the leaders of the organization take an approach to leadership, e.g., hands-on or hands-off, that aligns with your style?	✓	✓	
Leadership Also Producers Is your leadership in touch with the core business of providing insurance solutions to clients, or are they strictly executives?	✓	✓	
Community Involvement Does your company have a commitment to its community? How is it involved with the people?	✓ *Involved with many charities*	✓ *Involved with many charities and teams*	
Commitment to Employee/Team Health Is your company focused on the overall wellness of its employees? Are there extended programs that promote well-being?	✓	✓	
Mentors – for You Is there an opportunity to be mentored by senior executives?	✓	✓	

JOB COMPONENT	CURRENT MODEL	ENTREPRENEUR MODEL	DIFFERENCE
Opportunities to Mentor Is the company dedicated to the growth of its junior producers? Are there opportunities to participate in their growth?	✓	✓	
Noncompete/Restrictions Does your company have a noncompete? If so, how restrictive is it?	✓	None	
Freedom to Leave Does the company's leadership make it clear that it will work with you if you want to leave, regardless of a noncompete?	No	Yes	
Producer Retention Rate Does the company know their retention rate, and what is the percentage?	60%	99%	39%
Relocation Does working for the company mean that I will need to relocate?		No	
Negotiation for Transition Period Assistance If I have a noncompete and want to move, will the company work with me regarding finances during a transition period?		✓	Willing to work with my concerns

Chapter 4

SET REALISTIC EXPECTATIONS

If you're starting out from scratch without your prior book, it's probably going to take two or three years to get back to what you were making before you came over. This is normal, so embrace the process. As long as you're making steady progress toward your goal, you'll eventually get where you're going. Keep in mind, it's not just about the paycheck, it's also about the freedom to control your time. It's about the balance sheet side of the equation, too, where now you own a lucrative business with a marketable value of two times the annual revenue. With every account you write, you have a growing asset you didn't have before.

YOUR PIPELINE AND NETWORK ARE THE KEY

Whether you can buy your book outright or not, maintaining a full pipeline of qualified prospects is your key to success in transition and beyond. How do you keep your pipeline full?

Some producers, like Bruce Eades, prefer to become a niche specialist and fill their pipeline with prospects for which they have special expertise and a competitive advantage. When you focus on a niche, it becomes much easier to identify potential prospects, because you've already defined exactly what you're looking for. You can also offer special programs that solve their unique problems, get involved in their associations, develop targeted lists, reach them effectively via LinkedIn or other social media platforms, network with other vendors in the space, and so on.

Another successful producer, Nate Brainard, has served on several committees for the National Waste & Recycling Association (NWRA). By serving the association and its membership, he has gained unique insight into the industry, understands their challenges, and has become a trusted insurance advisor and "go to" expert in this niche.

Other producers, like Ali Pool, prefer to "fish where the fish are." In her area, there are lots of condo associations, so, guess what she's become an expert in? She's also served on numerous boards of directors. She volunteers her time and leverages her vast network of resources for helping others wherever and however she can. Like Nate, she chooses to "give first" without expecting anything in return. Rather than focusing on "what's in it for me," she always focuses on "what's in it for them." She's found that by doing this, the leads sort of just follow.

Some of our real estate specialists network with property managers and write property schedules all over the country. Use your surroundings to the best of your ability.

Conventional wisdom also says to network with CPAs and attorneys. While that's worked for some, it's never really worked for me. The best strategic networking relationships I have cultivated over the years are with employee benefits consultants (either within or outside of IOA), PEO reps, payroll reps, and outsourced CFOs. Since we've structured the relationships to be mutually beneficial, they have an incentive to keep me in mind and to send qualified referrals.

It really doesn't matter how you fill your pipeline or structure your network. If you maintain enough ongoing quality activity, you'll be in great shape.

SUPPORT ON THE HOME FRONT

Spousal or partner support is also crucial. Four or five months before I officially started at IOA, I started dating

Beth. We thought at the time it was temporary. She'd been recently divorced, too, so we often joked that we were each other's rebound. Eighteen years later, we're still together. It's the best relationship I've ever had. She's been by my side the whole time, and there's no doubt her support has enabled me to accomplish way more than I ever would have on my own.

Make sure your spouse or partner understands the big picture and shares your vision. If he or she doesn't fully understand the opportunity or appears hesitant, it sometimes helps to visit with some other successful producers and their spouses who have been through the same situation. At IOA, you will find many who are willing to share their experience.

FINDING BALANCE

Amid all this, it's essential to take care of yourself and try to maintain some balance in your life. For me, I've always been fairly well-balanced emotionally, but to maintain physical balance, I found that I need to eat healthy and hit the gym or do some form of exercise almost every day. My spiritual balance has come a long way and is still a work in progress. I find that listening to Joel Osteen or some other inspiring message while driving helps me maintain a positive outlook. It also reminds me that God is always in control and that I am not. I also attend a Friday morning men's Bible study, which has become the highlight of my week. I probably know less about the Bible than anyone there, but everyone is very supportive. The opportunity to hear a great message and talk openly with other authentic, like-minded men about real stuff is very inspiring.

Emotionally, physically, spiritually—you must have balance, and the more balanced your life is, the more successful you will be and the more energy you will have for building your business.

Chapter 5

ADDING VALUE TO THE INSURANCE TRANSACTION

At IOA, there are many tools to help you add value and grow your business.

RISKSCORE®

One tool we're very proud of is RiskScore.® It's a trade-marked proprietary system that systematically helps a company become more risk free. As a result, it reduces not just their insurance costs, but other costs and expenses over the long run, driving more profit to the bottom line—and it's only available through IOA. We've invested several million dollars, and our dedicated partners have invested thousands of hours getting it to where it is today. Major contributors also included thirty-one insurance company underwriters, numerous workers' compensation attorneys, and labor law attorneys.

In a nutshell, the score you get from RiskScore® is similar to a credit score, but it's for your business. It's a benchmark to show a company how they stack up compared with the best practices in their industry. The higher the score, the lower their risk, which translates into better rates and lower insurance costs.

One of our most successful producers, Rick Dalrymple, leads every new prospect conversation with RiskScore.® His approach is counterintuitive to the typical new business approach, and it's been wildly successful for him. When he meets with a company for the first time, he doesn't even mention the insurance policies. He explains that what they pay in premiums is only the tip of the iceberg. He then explains that their much larger costs are for other things that fall below the waterline, like the cost of a bad hire, the cost of attorney involvement, the loss of productivity, etc. All those things are much more expensive than the cost of the claims themselves.

When Rick sits down with a CEO, it quickly becomes apparent that their current agent is not having these types of conversations. Once you address and fix the expensive things, the insurance becomes kind of an afterthought. By introducing RiskScore,® Rick becomes a strategic partner, and his clients view him as a trusted advisor with a seat at the table along with their attorney and CPA.

CLAIM ADVOCACY

At IOA, we have a team of experienced in-house claim advocates who will make you look great and will turn your clients into raving fans. All of our advocates are licensed claims adjusters with an average of over fifteen years of experience. Whenever your client has a claim that requires some hand-holding or potentially some negotiation with the insurance carrier, you will have an awesome resource at your fingertips. In reality, most insureds depend on their agent to help with claims. However, most agents really aren't equipped to effectively negotiate claims and can get frustrated by the process.

A few years ago, one of my clients had a fire in their warehouse. Since our client was a tenant, the insurance carrier paid to clean the smoke damage to their inventory and equipment but denied any payment for cleaning the interior walls or interior office build-out. The carrier said that was the landlord's responsibility. The landlord cited a clause in the lease saying it was the tenant's responsibility. The carrier dug in firm on their position. After several months of hard work and taking it all the way up the management chain at the insurance carrier, our in-house claims advocate, Diane Gregg, was able to secure an additional payment of $94,000 for our insured to cover the balance of the cleanup. Her effort was invaluable to our client and something I could have never achieved on my own. Needless to say, our client has become a raving fan.

MOD ANALYSIS

We also provide advocacy in the area of experience mod analysis. Our mod analyst, Kelly Lopez, has been instrumental in helping me land and retain numerous accounts over the last eighteen years. Whether you're a seasoned veteran or new agent, she will find any errors and make you look like a true professional and a conscientious steward of your client's premium dollar. She also provides detailed reports including various what-if scenarios to help clients understand what's driving their cost and to help them make the smartest buying decision.

MARKET ACCESS

At IOA, you will have access to preferred relationships with most of the major national and regional carriers. You will be able to compete in most situations while bringing a superior product to the table.

LEARNING MANAGEMENT SYSTEM

We also have a Learning Management System (LMS) that we can provide for online employee training. Many companies pay thousands of dollars for their own LMS. The employees are trained in specific areas and then take a test. The system documents who has been trained on what and offers all relative data at your fingertips. It's an overall picture of what your employees have done and where each is at in the process. Having an LMS available to our clients means they don't have to pay for an outside vendor. They can just use ours.

We have hundreds of different courses, and we can add virtually any kind of training you could possibly want. You can roll it out to all your employees, know who's taken it, and see how they scored. You can essentially use it for all your ongoing training. We also provide our clients with comprehensive training on use of the LMS.

HR CONSULTING

At IOA, you will be able to provide both in-house and outsourced HR solutions to your clients, depending on the need. You will be able to offer basic services like an HR help desk and employee handbook design, or you can bring in an expert to assist with HR needs assessments/ audits, HR consulting, HR and leadership training, recruiting strategies and assistance, etc.

PRACTICE GROUPS

As we've grown, we've added producers who are experts in certain areas, so IOA has developed some internal practice groups. We've created groups charged with developing exclusive programs that provide specialized coverages and value-added services to the industries they serve. Clients benefit because they get the broadest coverage available in the industry provided by somebody who understands their business. Producers at IOA who become part of these groups are confident that they're bringing quality to the table, and they can gain expertise by working with the group.

The groups are at various stages of development. Some are fully functioning, and others are approaching completion. There are also some informal groups that leverage the expertise of specific producers to create a favorable advantage for the producer and client.

These groups include expertise in areas such as: architects and engineers, telecommunications, transportation, real estate, restaurants, environmental, construction, wrap up, cargo/throughput, aviation, agriculture, physician groups, waste hauling, government and defense contractors, temp staffing, etc. These will continue to expand as we add quality producers with additional areas of expertise.

These groups can benefit new producers or even veteran

producers looking for fresh inspiration or a new direction. If a producer isn't sure what opportunities to focus on, he or she can get involved with one or more of these groups and within a short time become an expert—and a lethal weapon in the marketplace.

Chapter 6

COLLABORATION INSTEAD OF COMPETITION

THE IOA SALES ACADEMY

As you know by now, at IOA, our producers don't compete with each other. We collaborate for the benefit of our clients, our insurance carrier partners, and ourselves. A great example of this is the IOA Sales Academy, which was developed by Jeremy Burr, one of our most successful producers. He's a super busy guy with a book of business well north of $1 million in annual revenue.

About ten years ago, he and one of our other top producers thought it would be a good idea to create a sales playbook available to everyone at IOA. The initial idea was to gather some of the most effective strategies for writing middle market-type accounts, put them in a format to share, and then distribute to the sales force.

It was initially a collaboration of ideas, but later evolved into the full-blown class as it exists today. The class runs for ten consecutive weeks and is available to anyone at IOA who wants to participate. Every year, the class draws a number of novice producers along with an impressive list of seasoned veterans eager to sharpen their skills. It covers a different topic each week and consists of a series of ten, one-hour conference calls. During the first half of the class, Jeremy teaches different fundamentals, which are taken from proven best practices of top producers. The second half of the class is my favorite part. Each week, there is a different superstar producer invited to speak as a guest. It's always someone who has achieved a high level of success and is eager to share from his or her experience. It's like getting personal mentoring from the most successful people in your field. And they aren't sharing mindless platitudes or blowing smoke like you'd hear in a typical sales course. They share authentically from the heart and are willing to personally help any one of us. I don't know anywhere else in our industry where a producer can gain such valuable understanding and insight.

When Jeremy decided to put together this class, he did it solely for the purpose of making a contribution. He receives no monetary compensation for doing it. While the preparation and execution takes a ton of his time, he is all about giving something back and making IOA a better place. They say, "It's not what you get that makes you happy, it's what you give." He gives a lot. He's gotten a lot in return, and it helps keep his skills sharp, too.

In addition, Jeremy has won our Partner of the Year award on several occasions, which is given out yearly at our annual sales conference. It recognizes the person responsible for making the greatest contribution not related to production. It's for a selfless contribution done for the greater good, to help others, and to make IOA a better place.

RETIREMENT SUCCESSION

Another way in which IOA helps producers collaborate is with formal succession in the event of retirement.

Let's face it. In our industry, the average producer is around fifty-five years of age and within that ten- to fifteen-year retirement window. At IOA, it's no different. About half of our producers are over age fifty. As a fifty-four-year-old with a large book, I used to think about this a lot. Especially since a large portion of my retirement income will depend on a well-executed succession strategy.

Fortunately, at IOA, I have complete freedom and flexibility to plan for this foreseeable event. While you can structure this any way you choose, I plan to transition out over time, while remaining as actively involved as I want. Through the IOA mentor program or an internal promotion, I will cultivate one or more mentees of my choosing to become my eventual successor. If I make good decisions and select those with the ability to retain and grow the business, everyone will win—the client, our carrier partners, the mentee, and myself. My book will be larger by the time I retire, which will result in a larger payout. The clients will have had time to get comfortable with my successor, meaning there should be little or no transition stress. The carrier partners can remain in place on the accounts. And my successor gets the benefit of having a solid foundation on which to continue building.

A great example of a successful transition is our president, Jeff Lagos. Years ago, Jeff was recruited to join IOA by veteran producer, Vern Duenow. Vern loved IOA and wanted to leave his clients in great hands upon his retirement. At the time, Jeff had worked in both underwriting and marketing positions with an insurance carrier but had never been a retail producer.

When Jeff came on board, Vern had a nice book of business, but it wasn't huge. After working with Jeff for eighteen months—and Jeff was good—they were able to increase the size of the book by 20 percent by the time Vern retired.

As a result, Vern was able to receive well over six figures more than what he would have received if he'd initially sold his book for two times revenue. Although Jeff had to pay more for the book, the transition was seamless for the clients and Jeff was making exponentially more than what he was pulling down on the carrier side.

Let me explain a bit more about how the mentor program works today.

THE IOA MENTOR-BROKER PROGRAM

With the aging producer population, there has never been a better time for a young person to enter the insurance business. Within the next ten to fifteen years, most of the wealth (books of business) will be transitioning from the current producers to the next generation. Of course, the only producers who will benefit are those working in an Entrepreneurial Model with the opportunity to own their book. For the young producer who can position himself or herself properly, the opportunity is virtually limitless.

The IOA Mentor-Broker program is a training platform designed to help do just that. It was established to encourage the growth of agents new to the insurance business by pairing them with an established, senior broker/producer. Its main purpose is to establish a defined perpetuation program for retiring producers and to bring new producers into IOA. It's a formal program that's been developed to help younger people and also provide an orderly, smooth transition for the retiring producers when the time comes.

For the younger producer, the program provides a well-defined approach for training. It outlines exactly what training he or she can expect. It's also a way for the inexperienced producer to enter the IOA system with little to no insurance experience. This is beneficial since they may have arrived from a completely different industry.

Within IOA, the program has some criteria for entry. In order to qualify to become a mentor, the producer must have a proven track record of success and must also have a current book of business of at least $500,000 in gross revenue. In a nutshell, the program gives new producers an opportunity to work closely with and learn from someone who's already been successful. Who better to learn from, right?

Both the mentor and mentee attend all meetings together including new prospect visits and renewal meetings with clients. It's a very hands-on process. This enables the mentee to learn from a practical standpoint how things should be handled, how to talk to clients, what questions to ask, etc.

The mentee's job is to sponge everything up, ask a lot

of questions, and learn the business over time. Our clients and prospects have responded well to the program. They seem to like the idea of teamwork and the youth being there as well. If they're considering going with IOA, they don't have to worry whether the agent is going to be around in five years.

In addition to the IOA Sales Academy and the hands-on mentor coaching, the mentee also receives world-class personalized training from Roger Sitkins, who brings his ProducerFit training program to IOA on an annual basis. Roger is considered by many to be the top insurance producer coach in the country. We'll also put the mentee through formal RiskScore® training, LinkedIn training, IOA University, etc. The mentee also has the opportunity to gain insight into specific industries via the different practice groups.

Our current group of mentees is super sharp. They routinely meet via conference call and exchange a free flow of ideas. It's kind of like pledging a fraternity or sorority. From your first day on campus, you're not alone. You instantly have a group of like-minded brothers and sisters who have your back and are willing to help with whatever you need. I would contrast this with one of our large national competitors that routinely encourages new producers to compete against each other.

To assist with the transition, there's also financing available in the form of a draw. It's an agreed amount per month and gives both the mentor and mentee some skin in the game. Mentors will cosign for the draw and are personally responsible for half of the balance. This ensures both will have a vested interest in the mentee becoming successful.

Even better, the commission split for the first-year mentee is extremely aggressive. We pay our mentees 90 percent of the commission on anything they write in the first year to give them a financial boost. If they're successful, they usually won't end up owing anything on the draw. We don't want them worrying about finances at a time when they should be learning and focused on growing their book. The mentee program is designed to be a three-year plan to get them ramped up. After three years, if they reach a certain level, the mentee is awarded his or her own, full-blown producer contract.

BEFORE TAKING THE FINAL LEAP

Here are a few final thoughts before you take the final leap.

Be ready for limited to zero supervision. Some find it helpful and motivating to stick to an established routine. Most of our producers opt to work in a branch office close to where they live. Each office has a support team, much like in the corporate environment. There's little difference except, at IOA, there's no sales manager cracking the whip or wondering when you're going to be in the office.

I always encourage people, especially when they're new, to ask a lot of questions, watch what other successful producers are doing, and then emulate their activity. It's not necessary to reinvent the wheel. Everyone's here to help. If you do well, we *all* do well. If you like to work from home, our technology allows you to do that. Make sure you're the kind of person who can do that and still be productive, not distracted.

David Hendrick is a great example of this. He works from home and frequently does so in his gym clothes on days when he's not seeing clients. He carries himself as if he's wearing his best suit and working in a skyscraper with IOA's name on it. He takes it that seriously. He has a dedicated office in his home and is always there between 8:00 a.m. and 5:00 p.m. on the days he works from there. Even though he could go and screw off, he doesn't because his clients depend on him and he's committed.

Another producer, Nick Altier, doesn't live close to a branch office, so he works from a remote office in Sarasota, Florida, all by himself. He dresses up in a suit and tie each day he goes in. He likes to suit up for battle, and it gives him confidence to go out and prospect. For him, suiting up makes a difference because it gets him in the right mindset.

When a producer comes to IOA from an environment where they've had a lot of structure, I encourage them to take some time to enjoy their newfound freedom because that's what it's all about. That's one of the biggest reasons you make the change: to enjoy some time with your family or take some time for yourself. We don't want you to solely focus on business. We want to build the life you want for yourself and your family and make it what you want. What does your dream life look like?

CONCLUSION

Experience the IOA Difference

Are you ready to experience something that looks different from anything else in the insurance industry? Here's a glimpse of what awaits you at IOA.

OUR PEOPLE

Our CEO, Heath Ritenour, always says, "What makes us so special is our people. I don't care what organization you're a part of, you're only as good as your people. And I will absolutely put our folks up line by line against anyone in our industry because they care and because they're advocates."

At IOA, you will find a strong team of supportive, family-oriented people. While we're a global company in scope, we have a smaller company feel. We are each other's family away from home.

When I think of our people, the first thing that comes to mind is how we make each other better. Something Joel Osteen frequently talks about is the importance of spending time with people who make us better. When we surround ourselves with people who build us up and inspire us to go further, there's no limit on what we can do and become.

They say we become the average of the five people we spend the most time with. If that's the case and we want to break through plateaus, we need to be around people who make a lot more than the level we're aspiring to get to. For example, if you want to make $100,000 a year, hang out with people who make at least $200,000 or $300,000. If you want to learn how to make $500,000, hang around with a bunch of people who make $700,000 to $1 million per year. All of a sudden, your barometer of success and expectations will reset.

At IOA, you will have the opportunity to meet and work alongside those who will help you reset your barometer of success and expectations.

OUR STORY IS STILL PLAYING OUT

Jon Thurman, IOA executive vice president, sums it up perfectly. He says IOA's story-in-the-making is significant to this industry—we attract people who want to be part of something much greater than themselves. IOA offers the opportunity to unleash the potential in one another, to serve one another, and to share and be affirming with one another. To integrate and live out our life's work.

Since IOA today is the smallest it's ever going to be again, I can hardly wait to see what the future holds and how our story continues to play out. In my personal opinion, the past is likely to repeat itself, and it will become something beyond what any of us ever expected or imagined.

BOTTOM LINE

I'll quote Heath Ritenour once again as he says, "In the midst of the daily grind, there really is no place like IOA. There is no other brokerage in America that gives you the ability to EARN and OWN like we do here. But you'll also add value and be part of a culture that actually cares."

Hence the inspiration for the name of this book, *EARN IT, OWN IT*.

So, what are you waiting for? Perhaps you're overthinking this and living the so-called analysis paralysis. I get it.

I've been there. But as I mentioned earlier, just get out a pen and paper and write out some worst-case scenarios. What's the worst you will do if you were to only write "X" amount of business in the first three or five years? How much income and equity would you have built?

Also ask yourself, what's the risk of not taking a shot? What's my freedom and independence worth? What regrets will I have ten years from now?

I think you'll discover there's little to lose and a whole lot to gain by making the move to IOA. Like Ali Pool said before making her move, "If you want something different, you need to do something different."

If you're afraid to take the risk, that's OK. There's no shame in playing it safe. I'm not saying that as a dig, either. The world needs great employees too. Everyone's not cut out to be the boss or run their own business. I know it sounds sexy to say, "I own my own business," or "I'm an entrepreneur." But, the reality is that it's a lot of hard work. It requires a level of consistent effort over time that most aren't willing to put in.

On the other hand, if you're not afraid of putting in some hard work in exchange for having a shot at living your dream life, come join us. There's a team of like-minded brothers and sisters waiting and eager to help you every step of the way. After all, we were all in your shoes once, and it's our obligation to pay it forward.

Remember, we're all in this together. When one of us succeeds, we all succeed.

Are you in?

ACKNOWLEDGMENTS

To my dad, Elmer Johnson. You've always been my biggest fan and source of encouragement. Without your unconditional love and support, I would have never had such amazing opportunities in life. The older I get, the wiser I realize you've always been.

To my best friend and partner in life, Beth. You've been by my side for this crazy journey over the last eighteen years. While it hasn't always been perfect, we've always been perfect together. Loving you along with our mutual love for helping others gives my life meaning.

Special thanks to my partners and teammates who graciously provided their time, assistance, and feedback for this book. You all personify the IOA spirit of giving and true partnership—and you inspire the hell out of me!

ABOUT THE
AUTHOR

BRUCE JOHNSON is a vice president, branch representative, and a top commercial producer with Insurance Office of America. He's a self-motivated sales entrepreneur, relentless client advocate, innovative problem solver, and humble servant leader.

His professional credentials include a business degree in risk management and insurance from Florida State University and a Chartered Property and Casualty Underwriter (CPCU) designation from The Institutes, which is held by less than 1 percent of commercial producers. He's been a licensed insurance agent since 1985 and has taught continuing education for various construction trade associations over the last fifteen years.

He has an intense curiosity for evolving technology and its effect on how we serve and deliver value to our clients. He also understands that we must constantly adapt and embrace new ideas in order to remain viable.

On a personal note, he's an avid believer with a passion for helping others. His interests include fitness, nutrition, traveling, boating, and FSU football. He's also a pickup-driving metro redneck with a black belt in kickboxing.

www.ingramcontent.com/pod-product-compliance
Lightning Source LLC
Chambersburg PA
CBHW031946190326
41519CB00007B/679